REVISED EDITION

Basics for Believers
AN INTRODUCTION TO CHRISTIAN GROWTH

JIM BERG

journey**forth**®

Greenville, South Carolina

All Scripture is quoted from the King James Version. Words or phrases in brackets are either substitutes for a word in the King James Version of the Bible or an additional word offered to make the meaning of the adjacent words clearer.

The fact that materials produced by other publishers may be referred to in this volume does not constitute an endorsement of the content or theological position of materials produced by such publishers.

Basics for Believers: An Introduction to Christian Growth, revised edition
Jim Berg

Cover illustration and design: Nathan Hutcheon
Illustration reference photo: istockphoto.com/shuchunke
Page layout: Michael Boone

© 1978, 2017 BJU Press
Greenville, South Carolina 29609
JourneyForth Books is a division of BJU Press.

ISBN 978-1-62856-349-8
eISBN 978-1-62856-350-4

15   14   13   12   11   10   9   8   7   6   5   4   3   2

CONTENTS

INTRODUCTION

Many people have looked upon Christianity as just another religion. Were it not for one basic difference, this might be true. Genuine Christianity is not a religion; it is a relationship. It is a relationship with Jesus Christ.

No one becomes a Christian by joining a church or being baptized or confirmed. One must personally know Jesus Christ (by experience) to be a Christian.

There is only one way to personally know Christ—by knowing and believing what God has told us about Him in God's Word, the Bible. In the Bible, God spells out the conditions that must be met before He accepts anyone into His family. It also tells us how to build our relationship with Him once we have become children of God.

If you are not a Christian or do not *know* whether you are, these simple Bible studies are for you. If you are a *new* Christian, these studies will help you to build your relationship with God. All you will need is some time alone, a pen or pencil, and a Bible. Read each verse carefully and prayerfully. Then answer the questions in your own words. In addition to the basic studies in Section One, several helps are included in Section Two.

God says that the most important thing in the world is that you know Him personally. Listen to what He says in Jeremiah 9:23–24:

> *Thus saith the Lord, Let not the wise man [boast] in his wisdom, neither let the mighty man [boast] in his might, let not the rich man [boast]in his riches: but let him that [boasts] [boast]in this,* that he understandeth and knoweth me.[1]

These studies can help you to *understand* and *know* the God of heaven.

---

[1]Words or phrases in [brackets] are either substitutes for a word in the King James Version of the Bible or an additional word offered to make the meaning of the adjacent words clearer.

How to Become a Christian[2]

A Crucial Question

Let me ask you a personal question. If you were to die today from a terminal illness or in some tragic accident and you were to stand before God, how would you answer God when He asked you this question: "Why should I let you into My heaven?"

Some people might feel that because they have been deeply religious and have obeyed the Ten Commandments[3] most of the time, God should let them into heaven. Others might feel that because they have lived by the Golden Rule[4] and have been honest and moral in their dealings with others, they should be allowed to enter. They are saying essentially that God should allow them to enter heaven because they have been good in some way.

Jesus predicted that many people who claim to be Christians would come to Him on that day and would say exactly those things. He says that His reply to them will be, "I never knew you: depart from me, ye that [practice sin]" (Matthew 7:23). No matter how many good things we have done, the factor that will keep us out of heaven is our sin.

The Bible makes it clear that "all have sinned, and come short of the glory of God" (Romans 3:23). That means that all of us have lived as if we are most important and that God doesn't matter. We instinctively place ourselves first instead of God and turn to our "own way" (Isaiah 53:6). Even our effort to get to heaven by being good shows our rebellion against God because He said that there is no way any of us can be good enough to merit heaven.

Every one of us has broken God's Ten Commandments—and have done so many times. He very clearly said that "the wages of sin is [eternal] death" (Romans 6:23). That means that all of us, because of our rebellion of going our own stubborn way in life, deserve the everlasting punishment of hell because of our mutiny against the Creator.

---

[2]Jim Berg, *When Trouble Comes* (Greenville, SC: BJU Press, 2002), 21–27.
[3]The Ten Commandments are found in Exodus 20:3–17.
[4]The Golden Rule, "Do unto others as you would have them do unto you," is a paraphrase of Jesus' statement in Matthew 7:12.

Good News

The good news for us is that eternal life—life in heaven with Jesus Christ forever—is not something we have to earn. It is a gift! Though "the wages of sin is [eternal] death . . . the gift of God is eternal life through Jesus Christ our Lord" (Romans 6:23). That is good news because the Bible also tells us that it is "not by works of righteousness which we have done, but according to his mercy he saved us" (Titus 3:5). God is willing to mercifully give us a gift we cannot earn. He wants to give us eternal life. But that gift must be personally received by us.

Many public meeting halls operate a lost-and-found area for those who use the facilities. The lost-and-found staff holds the property until someone comes by, identifies himself as the owner, and claims the item. Salvation from the eternal punishment of our sins is available to everyone, but we too must personally claim it.

How can salvation be a free gift? Though it is free to us, it cost Jesus Christ everything. You see, our sins against God require that a penalty be paid. Sinning against our Creator is such a great offense that the only just penalty is eternal suffering and separation from God Himself in hell. Hell is the result of God's granting a man his request—"God, leave me alone." We may not realize it, but that is essentially what we say to God every time we reject His way and live life our own way. That is the bad news for the sinner.[5]

The good news is that God loves us and arranged for His own Son to live on this earth to pay the penalty for us. Though Jesus lived in a body like ours, He did not share our sinful and stubborn nature. He lived a sinless life in complete obedience to His Father while on the earth. He qualified—as a perfect sacrificial lamb—to die in our place. Look at these chilling but wonderful words from the Old Testament, which predicted the sacrificial death of Jesus Christ on the cross for us:

> *But He was wounded for our transgressions, he was bruised for our iniquities: the chastisement [for] our peace was upon him; and with his stripes we are healed. All we like sheep have gone astray; we have turned every one to his own way; and the Lord hath laid on him the iniquity of us all. (Isaiah. 53:5–6)*

---

[5]Jesus Himself speaks of hell as a place of literal torment in Luke 16:19–31.

The apostle John states the same thing this way:

> For God so loved the world, that he gave his only begotten
> Son, that whosoever believeth in him should not perish,
> but have everlasting life. . . . He that believeth on him is
> not condemned: but he that believeth not is condemned
> already, because he hath not believed in the name of the
> only begotten Son of God. (John 3:16, 18)

Jesus' sacrifice of His own blood as the eternal payment for anyone who would believe on Him satisfied the righteous anger of God against our mutiny.

The Qualifying Transaction

An important transaction takes place at the time of our salvation that is the reason God can let us be with Him forever in heaven. The apostle Paul tells us about it in 2 Corinthians 5:21.

> For [God] hath made [Christ] to be sin for us, who knew
> no sin; that we might be made the righteousness of God in
> him.

That means that when Jesus died on the cross, He took all of the sin of the world on Him as if it were His own and paid the penalty for it by His death. God accepted that sacrifice on our behalf by raising Jesus from the dead.

When we come to Christ for salvation, God applies Christ's sin-payment to our account. But then He does something more! God credits all of Christ's own righteousness to our account, qualifying us for heaven. We enter heaven, not because we have done some good, but because we are fully righteous in the eyes of God because of Jesus Christ!

Paul talked about this again in Philippians 3:9, where he said that those who trust Jesus to save them are "found in him, not having [their] own righteousness, which is of the law, but that which is through the faith of Christ, the righteousness which is of God by faith."

Paul said that the perfect righteousness we must have to spend eternity with God in heaven is not found in keeping the laws of God (though a true believer will want to obey God), but is found in simply turning to Christ in repentance for sin and trusting Christ to save us.

What Next?

All that is left is for us to admit to God that we are indeed hell-deserving sinners, realize that Jesus died in our place and arose from the dead, and then accept the gift of eternal life from God. It is a simple plan— one that even a child can understand. A child will cry out for help to the person he believes will help him. A sinner who wants the gift of eternal life can come to Jesus Christ by praying a prayer like this:

> *Lord Jesus, I realize that I am a sinner. I have not obeyed You. I have gone my own way many times. Since You are perfect and Your heaven is perfect, I realize that even one sin would disqualify me from heaven.*
>
> *I repent[6] of my sin and ask Your forgiveness. I accept Your gift of eternal life. I want Your substitutionary death to be applied to my sin account, and I want the righteousness of Jesus to be applied to my account.[7] Cleanse me from my sin and make me one of Your own children.[8]*
>
> *Thank You for loving me and for saving me.*

It is our prayer that if you do not know Jesus Christ as your personal Savior from sin, you will repent of your sin and come to Christ today. He is waiting to hear from you. Here is what the apostle Paul says about God's desire for you to come to Him.

> *For whosoever shall call upon the name of the Lord shall be saved. (Romans 10:13).*

If this information is new to you, you may want to reread this first section several times, asking God to help you understand it. Of course, you don't have to understand it perfectly to continue working in this book. The chapters to come will help make this clearer to you.

---

[6]James 2:10.
[7]2 Corinthians 5:21.
[8]John 1:12.

SECTION ONE
Basic Studies

Eternal Life—Accepting God's Gift

People today are constantly making big promises. Television advertisements promise everything from whiter teeth to smoother-riding cars. All of these promises are trivial, however, when compared to the promise of eternal life that God offers to man.

It is sad that not every man has this eternal life. God's Word says that there are two groups of people in this world.

1. According to 1 John 5:11–12, what are these two groups?

   _____

   _____

2. What determines whether a person has eternal life or not (1 John 5:12)?

   _____

   _____

3. The Bible says that all men are sinners. In Romans 3:23 God declares that "all have sinned, and come short of the glory of God." Every man has broken God's law and deserves God's punishment. The Bible says that "the wages of sin is [eternal] death" (Romans 6:23). Even though man deserves to be punished for his sin, what did God do (John 3:16)?

   _____

   _____

4. Can a person do anything on his own to have eternal life (Titus 3:5)?

   _____

5. What must a person do to become part of God's family and have eternal life (John 1:12)?

   _____

   _____

6. Isaiah 55:7 says, "Let the wicked forsake his way, and the unrighteous man his thoughts." If a person truly desires to receive

Christ and have eternal life, according to this verse what will be his attitude toward sin?

_____

_____

_____

Note: A person who genuinely wants to be saved will express an attitude of repentance toward his sin. This means that he will not only acknowledge his sin (confess it to God), but he will be sorry enough about it that he will turn away from it.

7. What does God say about a person who has not received Christ and repented of his sin (John 3:18)?

_____

_____

8. Is it possible for a person to know whether or not he has eternal life (1 John 5:13)?

_____

9. Can you personally say, without hesitation, that you have God's gift of eternal life?

_____

10. If you answered *yes* to question 9 above, what reason(s) can you give for your answer?

_____

_____

_____

_____

For additional study about accepting God's gift of eternal life, see John 3:1–21.

Assurance—Believing God's Promises

Once a person repents of his sin and accepts God's gift of eternal life, Satan will begin to intimidate him and will try to cast doubts in his mind. This can be expected since Jesus called Satan the "father" of lies (John 8:44). Read the following promises carefully and note what God has said He will do when a person asks Christ to save him.

> *He that believeth on the Son hath everlasting life: and he that believeth not the Son shall not see life; but the wrath of God abideth on him.* (John 3:36)

> *And I give unto them eternal life; and they shall never perish, neither shall any man pluck them out of my hand.* (John 10:28)

> *Him that cometh to me I will in no wise cast out.* (John 6:37)

1. A lack of assurance can be an indication that you are not trusting God's promises. Have you ever repented of your sin and asked God to save you?

    _____

    Is it possible for God to lie or go back on a promise (Titus 1:2)?

    _____

    If God cannot lie and you have asked Christ to save you, what does John 5:24 say about you?

    _____

    _____

    _____

2. A lack of assurance can also mean that there is sin in your life that you have not confessed to God. It stands between you and God. What does Proverbs 28:13 say about the man who harbors sin in his life?

    _____

    If you have truly trusted Christ, you will forsake your sin; but should you sin, it is not necessary that you be saved again. You are already a member of God's family. He does not throw you out of the family, but He is disappointed and grieved over your sin. What does 1 John 1:9 say you are to do when you sin?

_____

What does this verse say that God will do?

_____

_____

_____

3. After you are saved, you begin to receive greater assurance as you see certain evidences in your life. Look up these verses below and note the evidences they describe.

   Romans 8:16 _____

   The Holy Spirit whispers to you, "You are my child."

   1 John 4:19—You find that you love _____

   1 John 3:14—You find that you love _____

   John 14:27—God gives you _____

4. According to 2 Corinthians 5:17, what should be happening to your old desires and ways?

   _____

   _____

5. Galatians 5:17—What is going on inside you now?

   _____

   _____

Each of these evidences indicates that you are God's child. They will grow as you feed daily on God's Word. To help you resist the doubts that Satan will send your way, cut out and memorize the verses on Memory Verse Cards 1 and 2 on page 24 of this book.

If after you have studied this chapter you still do not have a real assurance of your salvation, reread 1 John 5:11–13, study the chapter "Eternal Life—Accepting God's Gift" on pages 2–3 again, and reread "How to Become a Christian" on pages v–viii. You should also seek the help of another believer who is sure that he is saved. God desires that you feel secure in His family.

God's Word—Listening to God Speak

The Bible is a revelation of God's instructions to man. Since God Himself is the author, His Word possesses absolute authority over man. It touches on every area of life. In fact, the apostle Peter said that God's "divine power hath given unto us all things that pertain unto [eternal] life and godliness [in this life], through the knowledge of him [contained in the Bible] that hath called us to glory and virtue" (2 Peter 1:3).

That means that God has provided in the Bible all that we need to know about how to live fruitful and stable Christian lives. Jesus said, "Man shall not live by bread alone, but by every word that proceedeth out of the mouth of God" (Matthew 4:4).

There are countless benefits to be gained from reading and studying God's Word.

1. It is the source of the believer's faith.

   So then faith cometh by hearing, and hearing by the word of God. (Romans 10:17)

2. It reveals to us what God is like.

   We learn about someone else by listening to his words, watching what he does, and observing how he interacts with others. The same is true with God. The entire Bible is a revelation from God about Himself. We learn about Him by watching His actions, listening to what He says to us and others, and observing how He interacts with others. The entire Bible reveals God!

   My son, if thou wilt receive my words, . . . then shalt thou understand the fear of the Lord, and find the knowledge of God. (Proverbs 2:1, 5)

3. It gives us direction and understanding.

   Thy word is a lamp unto my feet, and a light unto my path. (Psalm 119:105)

   The entrance of thy words giveth light; it giveth understanding to the simple. (Psalm 119:130)

4. It gives victory over our sinful desires when we apply it.

   Thy word have I hid in mine heart, that I might not sin against thee. (Psalm 119:11)

   But God be thanked, that ye were the servants of sin, but ye have obeyed from the heart that form of doctrine

*[teachings in the Bible] which was delivered you. Being
then made free from sin, ye became the servants of righteousness.* (Romans 6:17–18)

Many other things can be said about the Bible. Read the following
questions and look up the answers in your Bible.

1. The Bible was written over a period of sixteen centuries by some
    forty men, yet all sixty-six books bear a remarkable unity. They
    teach the same salvation, the same moral standards, and they all
    point to the same Savior. Who guided the writers so that they all
    agree (2 Peter 1:21)?

    _____

    Note: This divine guidance of what the writers recorded is called
    inspiration.

2. What two statements about the Bible are given in 2 Timothy
    3:16?

    _____

    _____

3. What must we do to make the Bible personally beneficial
    (2 Timothy 2:15)?

    _____

4. What should be our attitude toward the Bible (Psalm 119:97)?

    _____

5. Job considered God's Word to be the most important thing in
    his life. How do we know this (Job 23:12)?

    _____

6. Why is it so important for new Christians to begin reading and
    studying the Bible right away (1 Peter 2:2)?

    _____

For additional study about listening to God speak, see Luke 8:4–15.
Read through "A Plan for a Daily Quiet Time with God" on pages 20–
21. This will give you some help in setting up a daily time of Bible
reading and application for your life.

Temptation—Resisting God's Enemy

A recently saved tribal chief was asked by a missionary how things were going in his new faith. The chief replied that he felt as if two dogs were fighting inside. The black dog wanted him to do evil, and the white dog wanted him to do right. When asked by the missionary which dog was winning, the chief replied, "The dog I feed the most."

The apostle Paul wrote of this same struggle when he said, "the flesh [sets its desires] against the Spirit, and the Spirit against the flesh: and these are contrary the one to the other: so that ye cannot do the things that ye would" (Galatians 5:17).

After a person becomes a Christian, he finds that God's Spirit is continually prompting him to do right. At the same time, his flesh[1] tries harder to tempt the believer to sin. Thus a continual and fierce battle rages. God's plan for overcoming the flesh is set forth in the Bible. Study the following passages carefully to learn how to resist the sinful desires of your heart.

1. Satan wants to destroy us by appealing to the sinful desires of our heart. What description of Satan is given in 1 Peter 5:8?

   _____

   _____

2. Hebrews 2:14 says that Christ rendered him powerless who "had the power of death, that is, the devil." Since Satan is a defeated enemy, what does God want us to be (Romans 8:37)?

   _____

3. The first battleground for most conflicts is the mind. What is a Christian to do when evil thoughts arise (2 Corinthians 10:5)?

   _____

---

[1]*Flesh* is the word the apostle Paul uses to describe the sinful desires of the human heart that continue to tempt us to sin even after we become Christians.

4. James 4:7 gives a two-fold plan for victory over Satan. List the two elements of this plan.

_____

_____

5. How did Jesus resist temptation (Matthew 4:4, 7, 10)?

_____

6. What did Jesus tell His disciples to do to resist temptations (Matthew 26:41)?

_____

7. Besides not allowing you to be tempted past your level of endurance, what does God promise to do for you (1 Corinthians 10:13)?

_____

8. What "way of escape" is described in 2 Timothy 2:22?

_____

9. If you should give in to temptation or fail to take the way of escape and find you have sinned, what should you do (1 John 1:9)?

_____

Read Psalm 139:23–24. Take a moment to ask God to examine your heart and mind. List below your areas of weakness. Find Bible verses from "Verses for Victory" on page 22 or find verses in other study helps and begin fortifying yourself against Satan's attacks.

Sins and Weaknesses	Verses for Victory
_____	_____
_____	_____
_____	_____
_____	_____

For additional help in resisting temptation, study Ephesians 6:10–18.

Prayer—Talking with God

Communication is the basis for every relationship. People who do not talk to each other never grow very close together. Reading the Bible and praying are the two basic activities for developing your relationship with God. Just as there are countless benefits from reading and studying God's Word, so there are untold blessings to be reaped through personal contact with God through prayer.

1. Prayer is the means of getting help in times of need.

    Let us therefore come boldly unto the throne of grace, that we may obtain mercy, and find grace to help in time of need. (Hebrews 4:16)

2. Prayer is the means of obtaining forgiveness of sins.

    If we confess our sins, he is faithful and just to forgive us our sins, and to cleanse us from all unrighteousness. (1 John 1:9)

3. Prayer is the means to spiritual strength.

    Men ought always to pray, and not to faint. (Luke 18:1)

4. Prayer makes God more real to the believer.

    Draw nigh [near] to God, and he will draw nigh to you. (James 4:8)

5. Prayer brings joy to the believer.

    In thy presence is fulness of joy. (Psalm 16:11)

6. Prayer is God's way of providing our needs.

    Ask, and it shall be given you; seek, and ye shall find; knock, and it shall be opened unto you. (Matthew 7:7)

7. Prayer is part of God's cure for worry.

    Be [worried about] nothing; but in everything by prayer and supplication with thanksgiving let your requests be made known unto God. And the peace of God, which passeth all understanding, shall [guard] your hearts and minds through Christ Jesus. (Philippians 4:6–7)

God's Word is full of promises to answer our prayers. However, along with each promise is a certain condition that God wants us to meet. State the conditions described in the verses to follow.

1. 1 John 3:22 (two conditions)

_____

_____

2. John 15:7 (two conditions)

_____

_____

3. John 14:13 _____
4. Mark 11:24 _____
5. 1 John 5:14–15 _____

   Note: We will know what is "according to His will" as we study the Word of God. The Holy Spirit helps us pray and "maketh intercession for the saints according to the will of God" (Romans 8:26–27).

Sometimes, however, it seems that God does not hear us. Sometimes He does not answer. In either case there is a reason. Look up the following references to discover some hindrances to prayer.

1. James 4:3
2. Isaiah 59:1–2 _____
3. Mark 11:25–26 _____

For additional help about talking with God, see Matthew 6:5–15.

Witnessing—Talking About God

What is a witness? A witness is one who has seen and heard something and has been called to testify about it before others.

One of the last things Jesus said before He ascended into heaven after His resurrection was, "ye shall be witnesses" (Acts 1:8). The early church took this to heart, and Christianity grew rapidly.

The responsibility to be a witness for Christ is every bit as heavy upon us today as it was in the first century. You may feel that you have not studied the Bible enough, but if you are a Christian, you can at least give someone else the testimony of how you were saved. The blind man in John 9 did not know much about Jesus either, but he knew that he had been changed. He said to the Pharisees, "Whether [Jesus] be a sinner or no, I know not: one thing I know, that, whereas I was blind, now I see" (John 9:25).

That simple testimony is enough for a start, but you will need to become familiar with Bible verses that will lend authority to what you say. Cut out Memory Verse Cards 3–8 on page 25 and begin to memorize them. Insert these verses into your personal testimony as you witness. Become familiar with the brief explanation of each verse given below.

Romans 3:23 (Card 3)	This verse means everyone has sinned. No one has measured up to God's standard of holiness.
Romans 6:23 (Card 4)	Because of our sin we deserve to spend eternity separated from God in hell—eternal death.
Ephesians 2:8–9 (Card 5)	There is nothing we can do to save ourselves. Salvation is a gift from God.
John 3:16 (Card 6)	God's great love for us caused Him to send His Son to die in our place and suffer our hell for us.
John 1:12 (Card 7)	We must believe Christ died for us and personally receive Him to have eternal life.
Isaiah 55:7 (Card 8)	God expects that if a man truly desires to be saved, he will turn from sin at the same time he turns to God.

1. What does Jesus promise to give you that will encourage you as you witness (Matthew 28:20)?

   _____

2. What did the early church pray for (Acts 4:29)?

   _____

3. Why is it so important to keep your life clean (Matthew 5:16)?

   _____

4. What are two results of leading someone to Christ (James 5:20)?

   _____

   _____

5. What does God say about the man who "wins souls"—tries to lead people to Christ—(Proverbs 11:30)?

   _____

   _____

Begin reading good books on sharing the gospel with the lost around you and become active in your church visitation program, if it has one. Take every opportunity that God gives to tell what God has done for you.

For additional help on talking about God, study the personal witnessing of Christ in John 3 as He talked with Nicodemus and in John 4 as He talked with the woman at the well.

Church Attendance— Meeting with God's People

In Acts 2:42 the Bible says that the new Christians "continued stedfastly in the apostle's doctrine [solid biblical teaching] and fellowship." These two elements are essential to Christian growth. God has established the local church as the means to meet these needs. Some today would scorn meeting together in an organized fashion. It is true that some churches have nothing to offer the believer who is seeking to be fed from God's Word, but God has not abandoned this institution. Of course, a Christian must use caution in selecting the right kind of church. God has chosen to use the church to build up His people. As long as a church stands true to God's Word, God will bless it and protect it.

1. According to Ephesians 4:11, God has set up certain types of Christian workers. One of these is the pastor. Verse 12 expresses the reason for his work. What is his purpose?

   _____

   _____

2. What is his responsibility according to Acts 20:28?

   _____

3. Some of the early believers in New Testament times had a certain problem. What was it (Hebrews 10:25)?

   _____

4. As Acts 2:42 points out, "fellowship" is essential to Christian growth. What benefit of fellowship does Ecclesiastes 4:9–10 describe?

   _____

5. What is another benefit of Christian fellowship (Hebrews 10:24)?

   _____

6. What is the proper attitude toward meeting with God's people to worship (Psalm 122:1)?

   _____

7. In contrast to fellowship with Christians, what is to be our response to ungodly friends (Proverbs 4:14)?

_____

8. Proverbs 13:20 says "he that walketh with wise men shall be wise." What does the rest of this verse say is the end of the man who does not seek Christian fellowship?

_____

Although it is important to attend church, a young believer must be selective in the church he attends. The Bible gives definite instructions as to the kind of church a Christian should fellowship with.

> Matthew 28:19–20—Its members must be concerned about reaching the unsaved for Christ both at home and around the world.
>
> 1 Corinthians 15:3–4—It must have the gospel as its central message. This means its pastors and teachers will continually be telling their listeners how to be saved. They may offer times of public "invitation" when a person can get help on how to be saved or may simply ask listeners to talk with them personally if they want to know more about how to become a child of God.
>
> 1 Timothy 3:1–13—Its leaders should meet God's qualifications of dedication and holy living.
>
> 2 Corinthians 6:14, 17—It should be independent of ungodly alliances and associations with religious organizations that do not obey the Bible or that do not *hold it to be entirely true* (inerrant). Churches that meet these qualifications often describe themselves as *independent, fundamental,* or *evangelical.* Once you find the right church, get involved in its ministries and attend all the services. God has raised up churches such as these to strengthen you spiritually through the Bible preaching and teaching and the fellowship with other believers who love and obey the Bible as you do.

In addition, the right kind of church will teach you from the Bible what you need to know about being baptized, giving financially to the Lord's work, and serving others in the church and in your community.

Dedication—Surrendering to God's Will

Once you repent of your sin and accept Jesus Christ as your Savior, you should soon realize that you are not your own. You belong to God. The apostle Paul said it this way:

> What? know ye not that your body is the temple of the Holy Ghost which is in you, which ye have of God, and ye are not your own? For ye are bought with a price: there-fore glorify God in your body, and in your spirit, which are God's. (1 Corinthians 6:19–20)

According to 1 Peter 1:18–19, what are we purchased with?

In Romans 12:1, Paul states that God wants us to present (give over) our bodies as a living sacrifice to Him. The picture Paul portrays here brings to mind the Old Testament sacrifices where an animal was killed and offered to God. Paul is saying that we are to be *dead* (sacrificed) yet *living*. We are to be alive physically, yet we are to consider ourselves dead to our flesh (our sinful nature). Romans 6:11 teaches this idea as well.

> Likewise [consider] ye also yourselves to be dead indeed unto sin, but alive unto God through Jesus Christ our Lord.

God wants you to allow Him to totally control your life since He owns you.

If you have not done so before, now would be a good time to bow your head and tell God that you want Him to have full control of you from this time on—you are now presenting your body to Him as a "living sacrifice." Also tell Him you recognize that since He bought you, He owns you; thus, you will do anything He wants you to do. This kind of submission is the daily heartbeat of all mature Christians. They want God to control everything in their lives. They live lives that are *dedicated*—set apart—for God. A prayer of surrender like this to God is something that you want to become a part of your daily experience with God.

After you have decided to surrender your body and life to God in this way, you will want to ask yourself, "What does God want me to do with my life now?" Here are several suggestions to consider.

1. Ask yourself, "What can I do for Christ now?"

   List the *opportunities* in your church where you may be able to serve (helping with the youth program, visiting shut-ins, service projects, etc.).

   _____

   _____

   _____

   _____

   List the *abilities*, *skills*, and *talents* that you have that can be used for God now.

   _____

   _____

   _____

   _____

   In what ways can you be a *testimony* for Christ?

   At home _____

   _____

   _____

   At work/school _____

   _____

   _____

2. Ask yourself, "What can I do for Christ in the future?"

   Has God placed on your heart a burden for a particular type of work or Christian service?

   _____

   If so, what is it? _____

   _____

   Are you willing to serve God anywhere? _____

   Do you need additional educational preparation? _____

Note: Often someone who has recently been saved finds it helpful to prepare for service at a Christian school. Ask your pastor for a recommendation.

In Proverbs 3:5–6 God promises to "direct [your] paths" if you "acknowledge him" "in all [your] ways." May God bless you as you seek to find and do His will.

For additional help about surrendering to God's will, see Luke 9:23–26.

SECTION TWO
Additional Helps for Christian Growth

A Plan for a Daily Quiet Time with God

Nothing will help you grow more and build your relationship with God more quickly than a daily quiet time. This is a time when you meet with God. Remember the following points as you begin to make this a part of your daily schedule.

1. Establish a *regular* time. Many Christians find that early morning is best since their first thoughts can be of spiritual things (Psalm 5:3).

2. Get alone. Shut yourself up in a room away from the distractions of people if possible (Matthew 6:6) and resist the distractions of social media and of texting during this private time with God.

3. Have a pen and notebook ready. Proverbs 10:14 says, "Wise men lay [store] up knowledge." Be ready to write down anything that God points out to you from His Word. This is often called journaling.

You should include the following elements in your quiet time.

1. Bible reading

   Pray before you begin reading. Ask God to show you something just for yourself (Psalm 119:18).

   Follow a Bible reading schedule so that your reading is not haphazard. If you are a new Christian, first begin by reading 1 John, the Gospel of John, and James, then go back and finish the rest of the New Testament. Some find that including the chapter of Proverbs that corresponds to the day of the month is helpful too. (Read Proverbs 15 on the fifteenth day of the month, etc.) Or you might want to follow the reading schedule on page 23.

   Read until God points out something especially for you. Jot down the verse in your journal and your immediate thoughts about it. As you read, God will convict you of sins in your life. Write down your decision to forsake these sins. Confess these to God and ask for power to overcome them in your prayer time. God uses His Word to cleanse us (John 15:3).

   Thank God for what He has shown you in your reading.

   Share these special verses and insights with others (1 John 1:3).

2. Meditation—4M Formula

> *Mark* verses in your Bible from the "Verses for Victory" listed on page 22 or from your own Bible reading and write them out on cards to carry with you.
>
> *Memorize* these verses in free moments during the day (Psalm 119:11).
>
> *Meditate* on one verse or passage for a few minutes during your quiet time (Psalm 1:2–3). In meditation you are thinking of applications of these verses to your life. You are "personalizing" God's Word.
>
> *Master* these Bible truths in your daily life. God will bring opportunities into your life for you to "exercise" and grow stronger (Hebrews 5:14).

3. Prayer—Keep a personal prayer journal

Our prayers to God should contain a balance of praise, confession, thanksgiving, and supplication (asking). You can keep this balance by letting the word "PRAY" remind you of these elements. Memorize the Scripture passages following each component and pray them back to God from the depths of your heart. Record your prayer requests in your journal with the date of the request and the date of the answer.

> **P**raise—What did God do for you recently or show you from His Word today for which you can praise Him (Psalm 8; 1 Chronicles 29:11–13)?
>
> **R**epent—What has God shown you today that you need to confess and forsake (1 John 1:9; Psalm 32:1–5)?
>
> **A**sk—What do you need to ask God to do for you or for someone else today (Matthew 7:7–11; Hebrews 4:14–16)?
>
> **Y**ield—Where do you need to humble yourself to God and give up something you are stubbornly holding on to (James 4:6–10)?

A balanced prayer life includes all of these components. Our tendency is to forget the times of praise. Without it, however, our prayer life becomes a shallow "give me" time. Your times of praise and thanksgiving will become easier as you see God answer your requests. Of course, this does not mean that every time you pray you must include all four elements, but none of them should be missing from your regular prayer life.

Verses for Victory

Assurance	John 3:36	John 10:28	1 John 5:13
Christian Walk	Ephesians 4:1, 2	Ephesians 5:2	Ephesians 5:8–9
Church Attendance	Psalm 122:1	Matthew 18:20	Hebrews 10:25
Courage	Psalm 31:24	Psalm 34:4	Proverbs 29:25
Critical Spirit	1 Corinthians 10:10	Philippians 2:14	James 5:9
Evil Thoughts	2 Corinthians 10:5	Ephesians 5:12	Philippians 4:8
Forgiveness	Psalm 103:12	1 John 1:9	1 John 2:1–2
Forgiving Others	Matthew 5:44	Mark 11:25	Ephesians 4:32
Guidance	Psalm 32:8	Proverbs 1:23	Proverbs 3:5, 6
Knowing God	Jeremiah 9:23–24	John 17:3	Philippians 3:8, 10
Love	Deuteronomy 6:5	John 13:35	John 15:13
Lust (1)	2 Timothy 2:22	1 Peter 2:11	1 John 2:15–17
Lust (2)	Matthew 5:28	Romans 13:14	James 1:14–15
Lying	Psalm 101:7	Psalm 120:2	Proverbs 19:5
Patience	Hebrews 10:36	James 1:2–4	1 Peter 2:20
Peace	John 14:27	John 16:33	Philippians 4:6–7
Pleasing God	Matthew 6:5–6	Ephesians 6:6–7	Colossians 3:23
Pride (1)	Proverbs 16:18	Romans 12:3	James 4:6
Pride (2)	Obadiah 1:4	Matthew 20:26–27	1 Corinthians 4:7
Priorities	Matthew 6:33	Acts 20:24	Philippians 3:8
Self-Discipline	Ecclesiastes 5:4	Luke 9:23	James 1:19–20
Stealing	Exodus 20:15	Proverbs 30:8–9	Ephesians 4:28
Strength	Ephesians 3:16	Ephesians 6:10–11	Philippians 4:13
Strong Drink	Isaiah 5:11	Habakkuk 2:15	Romans 14:21
Suffering	Romans 8:18	Philippians 1:29	1 Peter 2:21
Temptation	Romans 6:11–13	1 Corinthians 10:13	James 4:7
Tongue	Prov. 10:19	Eph. 4:29	James 3:6
Wise Counsel	Proverbs 1:5	Proverbs 11:14	Proverbs 12:15
Worldliness	Romans 12:2	Colossians 3:2	James 4:4

As you find other areas of need and Verses for Victory write them below
or in your journal.

_____

_____

_____

_____

_____

_____

Bible Reading Schedule for the New Testament

Date read		Date Read	
_____	Matthew 1–4	_____	Acts 12–13
_____	Matthew 5–7	_____	Acts 14–15
_____	Matthew 8–10	_____	Acts 16–18
_____	Matthew 11–12	_____	Acts 19–20
_____	Matthew 13–14	_____	Acts 21–23
_____	Matthew 15–17	_____	Acts 24–26
_____	Matthew 18–20	_____	Acts 27–28
_____	Matthew 21–22	_____	Romans 1–3
_____	Matthew 23–24	_____	Romans 4–7
_____	Matthew 25–26	_____	Romans 8–11
_____	Matthew 27–28	_____	Romans 12–16
_____	Mark 1–3	_____	1 Corinthians 1–4
_____	Mark 4–5	_____	1 Corinthians 5–8
_____	Mark 6–7	_____	1 Corinthians 9–11
_____	Mark 8–9	_____	1 Corinthians 12–14
_____	Mark 10–12	_____	1 Corinthians 15–16
_____	Mark 13–14	_____	2 Corinthians 1–5
_____	Mark 15–16	_____	2 Corinthians 6–10
_____	Luke 1–2	_____	2 Corinthians 11–13
_____	Luke 3–4	_____	Galatians 1–4
_____	Luke 5–6		Galatians 5–Ephesians 3
_____	Luke 7–8	_____	Ephesians 4–6
_____	Luke 9–10	_____	Philippians 1–4
_____	Luke 11–12	_____	Colossians 1–4
_____	Luke 13–15	_____	1 Thessalonians 1–5
_____	Luke 16–18	_____	2 Thessalonians 1–3
_____	Luke 19–20	_____	1 Timothy 1–6
_____	Luke 21–22	_____	2 Timothy 1–4
_____	Luke 23–24	_____	Titus–Philemon
_____	John 1–2	_____	Hebrews 1–4
_____	John 3–4	_____	Hebrews 5–8
_____	John 5–6	_____	Hebrews 9–10
_____	John 7–8	_____	Hebrews 11–13
_____	John 9–10	_____	James 1–5
_____	John 11–12	_____	1 Peter 1–5
_____	John 13–15	_____	2 Peter 1–3
_____	John 16–18	_____	1 John 1–5
_____	John 19–21	_____	2 John–Revelation 2
_____	Acts 1–2	_____	Revelation 3–8
_____	Acts 3–5	_____	Revelation 9–13
_____	Acts 6–7	_____	Revelation 14–18
_____	Acts 8–9	_____	Revelation 19–22
_____	Acts 10–11		

Instructions for Memory Verse Cards

These Scripture verse cards are to help you as you memorize the verses in the studies on Assurance and Witnessing. Cut the cards out or photocopy them and carry them with you so that you can learn and review them in spare moments during the day.

7. We must believe on Christ

But as many as received him, to them gave he power to become the sons of God, even to them that believe on his name.

John 1:12

8. We must turn from sin

Let the wicked forsake his way, and the unrighteous man his thoughts: and let him return unto the Lord, and he will have mercy upon him; and to our God, for he will abundantly pardon.

Isaiah 55:7

4. The penalty of sin

For the wages of sin is death; but the gift of God is eternal life through Jesus Christ our Lord.

Romans 6:23

5. We cannot save ourselves

For by grace are ye saved through faith; and that not of yourselves: it is the gift of God: not of works, lest any man should boast.

Ephesians 2:8–9

1. Assurance

He that believeth on the Son hath everlasting life: and he that believeth not the Son shall not see life; but the wrath of God abideth on him.

John 3:36

2. Assurance

And I give unto them eternal life; and they shall never perish, neither shall any man pluck them out of my hand.

John 10:28

6. Christ died for us

For God so loved the world, that he gave his only begotten Son, that whosoever believeth in him should not perish, but have everlasting life.

John 3:16

3. We are all sinners

For all have sinned, and come short of the glory of God.

Romans 3:23